...You can't stop the wind blowing - you can only add to the gale.

Charlie Watson

1999

GW00706067

Girls don't fart...

A class-mate once told me that girls never fart
And always stay windless and pure,
But, having conducted research on my sis'
I seem to have found a good cure:
A portion of bran flakes for breakfast
A platter of lentils for tea,
A little control of the colon
And some careful instruction from me.

The Impish Verse Series

Burps & Farts

by Charlie Watson

Illustrations by Richard Lowdell

Nightingale

An imprint of Wimbledon Publishing Company
LONDON

Copyright © 2000
Illustrations © 2000 WPC

First published in Great Britain in 2000
by Wimbledon Publishing Company Ltd
P.O. Box 9779 London SW19 7ZG

First published 2000 in Great Britain

ISBN: 1903222 12 5

Produced in Great Britain
Printed and bound in Hungary

Burps

and Farts

You will know when maturity has finally claimed you, the day someone farts in your presence and you take offence. That is the start of the slippery slope into propriety and decency. No one has fun there. Let's be honest, we all need to let rip at some stage. We can't always let it seep out discreetly or find a quiet corner when we need to do so. And the truth is, the more people try to disguise the natural functions of the body, the more the body finds different ways of expressing itself. These poems aim to depict the most common expulsions and force people to stare the truth in the eye...

Smelly Toilets

A friend of mine advised me
'After going for a poo,
A flame will kill the odour
When it's held above the loo.'
Perchance he had forgotten
All the methane I emit,
The loo's now got no ceiling
Thanks to one match that I lit.

The Clumsy Jester

Those that fart quite publicly
And like to play the clown,
Probably undress to find
Their undies peppered brown.

The Big Release

I pity those that feel it wrong
To part their cheeks and parp,
They'll never know the pleasure
Of a deep, resounding fart,
That empties every inch of gut
From gales that brew inside,
And causes those within a mile
To scatter, run and hide.

The Nervous Squeak

Last week I was called for a meeting
With Cuthbert, Carmicheal & Shaw,
In pin-stripes and braces I figured
I'd forge out my future in law.
But just as the questions were starting
A rumbling of nerves in my tum,
Until I was asked, 'Any questions?'
And the first one was posed by my bum.

The Untimely Emission

Having had curry the night before work
The reverend felt like he'd sinned,
The next day in church he just hoped to dear God
That his cassock would keep in the wind.
The service of marriage was going quite well,
The vows of commitment had started,
'Til 'Do you take Gladys to have and to hold?'
Was greeted by, 'Jesus! Who's farted?'

Silent but Violent

A fine fart is more than mere fanfare and noise
It needs a fine-balanced aroma,
And even a whisper that scarce can be heard
Can put a grown man in coma.
This furtive emission can strike with surprise
Its warning signs easily missed,
The eyes should observe a slight cock of the cheeks
The ears should detect a faint hiss.

The Royal Trumpet

Even the Queen emits wind now and then
I know it sounds strange but it's true,
Even Her Majesty makes whoopee sounds
When straining to let out a poo.

The Wet Fart

Although it is prudent to stifle your farts
This method can land you in trouble,
We all should take care when the vapour creeps out
Encased in a brown liquid bubble.
The wet fart is harmless when naked and free
But harsh when the bum is contained,
It's double the shame for those caught unawares
With pride and pants horribly stained.

Lover's Games

My girlfriend gets angry if forced to inhale
My smells even though I'm her lover,
At bed-time I strive hard to muffle my farts
Then rouse her by wafting the cover.

Passing the Buck

Bank robbers, murderers, traitors and thieves
The hangman alone can correct 'em,
But worse even still is the man who lets rip
Then censures another man's rectum.

The Contented Belch

In terms of English etiquette
A belch is an infraction,
Although I've heard in Arab lands
A burp shows satisfaction.
Perhaps here too we all should
Tailor burps for what we eat,
On second thoughts the burp
For my Mum's roast would last a week.

The Concealed Burp

Why do people burp and hold
A hanky to their face?
As if this silk material
Could bring a touch of grace,
To all the bits of soggy food
That just don't want to die,
And echo from your stomach
With a sad and plaintive cry.

The Tactical Belch

A handy tip for gluttons:
A burp makes vital space,
So excess bits of swallowed food
Can find a resting place.
I've used the 'belch-and-gulp' approach
When eating at my Mum's,
I seem polite and finish
Though each plateful weighs three tonnes.

The Belching Sexes

Girls often burp like a rainforest frog
A croak that appears soft and sweet,
Men on the other hand, see every belch
As a splendid and wonderful feat.
When a girl burps it's but an admission
That 'even young ladies succumb',
When a guy burps it's only a warm-up
For thunders that lurk in his tum.

Stuck in the Back of the Throat

It's best to avoid the condition
That leaves you with mouth half-agape,
Suggesting a fault in the gullet
Has meant that a belch can't escape.
It's awkward, but easily dealt with
Providing you don't burp too soon,
Just gobble towards indigestion
Then let out the gas in a BOOM!

Toilet Humour

I fail to understand the prudes
Who don't find trumping funny,
Who do not love the belch or sneeze
Or rumble in the tummy.
These sober few don't understand
Though seeming old and wise,
That most of us enjoy our farts
Because we get a rise.

Bubbles in the Bath

Though you lose the raspberry
In the bath-tub when you fart,
By God you get a great bouquet
When watered buttocks part!

Elevator Fart

There are a few locations
That are perfect for the farter,
Providing just the context
For a little childish laughter.
A crowded tube, a silent lift
A church - all three are great,
To drop a bomb and point,
So people glower at your mate.

Alternative Medicine

I don't require an enema
To flush my botty hole,
I don't do yogic breathing
When I cleanse my inner soul,
Instead I have a plate of beans
And sit down with a brew,
So I can belch and then fart out
The gases I accrue.

Winding

Babies have the nicest life
Their burping is applauded,
And just a little gurgle is
Immediately rewarded.
If only some things didn't change
And winding never ceased,
And all my loved ones rubbed my back
To spur a great release.

Fart Control

I met a crazy Englishman
Who'd suck wind in his belly,
Then fire at will a bottom burp
With style, panache and welly.
'God damn!' I lauded, awe struck,
'That is a skilful ass!'
'A bum that saves on bills,' he said,
'I don't need British Gas.'

The follow-through

There's more to pets and children
Than just their being cute,
They can't perform the simplest belch
And often bring up puke.

The Friendly Fart

Apparently animals deem it polite
To sniff out the bum of a friend,
But manners like this are lost on my mates
Who can't see the warmth I intend,
My brother for instance will always deny
My animal right to commune,
Whenever I offer my bum for a sniff
He runs like a girl from the room.

The Raspberry

God makes us poop to ensure that we laugh
Whenever this strange noise is heard,
Divine intervention reminding us all
How deep-down our lives are absurd
And while we mature and our vanity grows
The raspberry's meant to impart,
The innocent humour we had in our youth
When our wittiest gag was a fart.

Expressions of Love

I think it strange I'm most polite
To those I hardly know,
Whilst to my friends the standard
Signs of love I cannot show.
I can't swear at a stranger
But make fun of my mates,
And only show a friend my love
By belching in his face.

The Orchestra

Although it's fine and dandy to
Stay alone and fart,
The flatulent require a group
To hone their special art.
The strangest thing about these bands
That typifies each tune,
Is every person has to play
The part of the bassoon.

The O-zone

The farts of Australian sheep
Are said to paralyse,
All who step behind the bum
Before the volley flies.
And now above the continent
The o-zone has been thinned,
'Coz all the lambs down under
Have such a toxic wind.

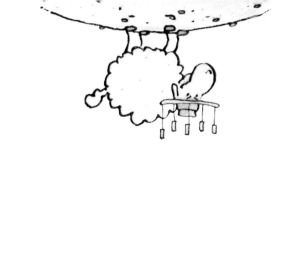

Bye!